SAXON MATH

Intermediate 4

Test-Taking Strategies Guide

Stephen Hake

A Harcourt Achieve Imprint

www.SaxonPublishers.com
1-800-284-7019

ISBN 13: 978-1-6003-2493-2
ISBN 10:   1-6003-2493-2

© 2008 Harcourt Achieve Inc.

Saxon is a trademark of Harcourt Achieve Inc.

Printed in the United States of America.

4 5 6 7 8 862 15 14 13 12 11 10 09

Table of Contents

To the Teacher

Saxon Math Test-Taking Strategies Guide provides an opportunity for students to practice their mathematical skills prior to taking your state's standardized test, which is based on an established measure of satisfactory performance.

Your state will define what students should know by the end of the academic year at each grade level. This book includes practice with these student expectations for grade 4 mathematics.

A review of your state's student expectations for grades 3 and 5 can help provide a broader context for your state's grade 4 standards.

Assessment and Your State

Student performance in different curriculums is often assessed by state tests. To further prepare your students for these tests, please see your state's educational website. This website may be a useful tool for understanding your state's test and specific objectives. Many states also provide more information and resources, including booklets, which offer additional clarification.

Most state standards prescribe overall objectives that are further defined by smaller subsets of student expectations. *Saxon Math* Test-Taking Strategies Guide will include a variety of samplings to provide practice in these subsets.

Sometimes students understand a math concept and can perform to expectation but will miss a question. This may happen because the standardized test presents the concept in an unfamiliar way or states the problem using unfamiliar vocabulary. *Saxon Math* Test-Taking Strategies Guide presents strategies to help students overcome these issues. After completing these practice tests:

- Students will be familiar with the specific language used on tests.
- Students will know the mathematical processes used on tests.
- Students will recognize the presentations and figures used on tests.

Saxon Math Test-Taking Strategies Guide provides practice problems designed to help your students prepare for test day. The multiple-choice problems and gridded-response problems are similar in format and content to what students will see on your state's test. A variety of questions will be presented throughout this book.

The Practice Test

The practice test will allow you to identify skills and concepts that students may need to review, practice, or be retaught to build better comprehension.

Teacher tips and student tips are provided to help you effectively administer the practice test.

Preparing Students for the Mathematics Test

- Review your state's objectives and the student expectations for grade 4.

- Incorporate your state's objectives in your lesson plans throughout the school year.

- Explain the purpose of the Practice Test to your students, such as enhancing confidence, boosting performance, and improving test-taking skills.

- Use released test items (if available) as extra-credit assignments or as bonus questions on routine tests throughout the school year. This will familiarize students with the format and content of the test.

- Give the Practice Test as part of your preparation for your state test in an environment similar to that of your state's testing environment.

- Review Practice Test questions and answers with students and analyze Practice Test results to identify students' strengths and weaknesses.

- Develop a teaching plan to address identified gaps.

Teacher Tips for Administering the Practice Test

- Prior to the Practice Test, review test-taking strategies with your students.

- Review the Grade 4 Math Vocabulary List (page 8).

- Remind students that the Practice Test is similar in content and format to the state test.

- Familiarize students with their state's testing environment by reviewing and following the same rules and procedures as those that students will experience on test day.

- Remind students that the use of calculators is NOT allowed on the Practice Test.

- Provide enough time for students to carefully read all instructions and to ask questions before beginning the Practice Test.

- Be sure students have two sharpened No. 2 pencils with erasers before they begin the Practice Test.

- Encourage students to check all answers carefully to make sure they are reasonable. One way to check is to compare an answer to an estimate.

- Encourage students to write out all calculations in the space provided to help them identify errors before choosing answers. Students are not allowed to use separate scratch paper.

- Alert students that the Practice Test contains many figures and that some figures may be for illustration only.

- Tell students to record their answers on the separate answer document carefully. Make sure students understand how to record their answers using the answer document (demonstrate if necessary).

- Encourage students to "take their time" but to not spend too much time on any one problem. Remind students that they can always come back to difficult questions later.

- Remind students that if they skip difficult questions, they should pay close attention to which answer space they are using on the Answer Document.

- Tell students they should continue working until they see the "STOP" sign on the last page.

Independent Strategy Practice Answer Key

Where students are asked to provide explanations for their choices, student responses will vary. Sample responses are given below.

Page 10
1. D
2. H
3. A
4. G

Page 12
5. A
6. J
7. C
8. J

Page 13
Multiply 18 and 6. Then compare the product to your estimation to see if it is reasonable.

Page 14
9. C
10. F
11. C
12. H

Page 15
$\underline{8} \div 2 = 4$;
$21 \div \underline{3} = 7$;
$30 \div \underline{5} = 6$

Page 16
13. A
14. H
15. D
16. G

Page 18
17. D
18. J
19. A
20. G

Page 20
21. B
22. H
23. A
24. G

Page 22
25. C
26. J
27. A
28. F

Page 23
432 inches;
72 times

Page 24
29. C
30. G
31. D
32. F

Page 26
33. C
34. J
35. A
36. H

Page 27

$\dfrac{1}{2}, \dfrac{4}{4}$

Page 28

37. **D**
38. **F**
39. **C**
40. **H**

Page 29

Count the completely shaded, large squares. There are 3. Then count the small, shaded squares in the partially shaded, large square. There are 56 small squares shaded out of 100 small squares. This is the same as 3.56.

Page 30

41. **A**
42. **H**
43. **D**
44. **J**

Page 31

Rounding each price to the nearest 50¢ will simplify the problem.

$3.49 ⟶ $3.50
$2.99 ⟶ $3.00
$1.99 ⟶ $2.00

These numbers are easier to add.

Page 32

45. **C**
46. **F**
47. **D**
48. **J**

Page 33

4 points

Page 34

49. **B**
50. **H**
51. **A**
52. **F**

Page 36

53. **B**
54. **J**
55. **D**
56. **G**

Page 37

All three figures are closed, flat shapes with straight edges; middle figure–octagon; right–hexagon.

Page 38

57. **B**
58. **J**
59. **A**
60. **H**

Page 39

The whole number stays the same. One place to the right of the decimal point is the tenths place. To convert the decimal to a fraction, delete the decimal point and use 6 as the numerator and 10 as the denominator. The fraction would be $2\dfrac{6}{10}$.

Page 40

61. **B**
62. **J**
63. **C**
64. **F**

Page 41

F is a translation;
H is a rotation;
J is a translation.

Page 42

65. **B**
66. **F**
67. **B**

Answer Document

Student's Name:

LAST | FIRST | MI

School: **Teacher:**

Fill-in your answer choice completely using a No. 2 pencil.

Samples:

A. Ⓐ ● Ⓒ Ⓓ
B. Ⓕ ● Ⓗ Ⓙ

1. Ⓐ ● Ⓒ Ⓓ
2. Ⓕ Ⓖ ● Ⓙ
3. Ⓐ Ⓑ Ⓒ ●
4. ● Ⓖ Ⓗ Ⓙ
5. Ⓐ ● Ⓒ Ⓓ
6. Ⓕ Ⓖ ● Ⓙ
7. ● Ⓑ Ⓒ Ⓓ
8. Ⓕ ● Ⓗ Ⓙ
9. Ⓐ ● Ⓒ Ⓓ
10. ● Ⓖ Ⓗ Ⓙ
11. Ⓐ Ⓑ ● Ⓓ
12. Ⓕ ● Ⓗ Ⓙ
13. Ⓐ Ⓑ Ⓒ ●
14. Ⓕ Ⓖ Ⓗ ●
15. Ⓐ ● Ⓒ Ⓓ
16. ● Ⓖ Ⓗ Ⓙ
17. Ⓐ ● Ⓒ Ⓓ
18. Ⓕ ● Ⓗ Ⓙ
19. Ⓐ Ⓑ Ⓒ ●
20. Ⓕ Ⓖ ● Ⓙ

Instructions:

1. Write your name in the space provided.
2. Be sure the problem number you are working on matches the answer number for each answer you fill in.
3. If you are taking the **Practice Test**, when you reach question 21 use the numbers in the gridded-response box.

21.

			1	.	8	3
⓪	⓪	⓪	⓪		⓪	⓪
①	①	①	●		①	①
②	②	②	②		②	②
③	③	③	③		③	●
④	④	④	④		④	④
⑤	⑤	⑤	⑤		⑤	⑤
⑥	⑥	⑥	⑥		⑥	⑥
⑦	⑦	⑦	⑦		⑦	⑦
⑧	⑧	⑧	⑧		●	⑧
⑨	⑨	⑨	⑨		⑨	⑨

22. ● Ⓖ Ⓗ Ⓙ
23. Ⓐ ● Ⓒ Ⓓ
24. Ⓕ ● Ⓗ Ⓙ
25. Ⓐ Ⓑ Ⓒ ●
26. Ⓕ Ⓖ Ⓗ ●
27. Ⓐ ● Ⓒ Ⓓ
28. Ⓕ Ⓖ ● Ⓙ

29. Ⓐ ● Ⓒ Ⓓ
30. Ⓕ Ⓖ Ⓗ ●
31. Ⓐ Ⓑ ● Ⓓ
32. ● Ⓖ Ⓗ Ⓙ
33. Ⓐ Ⓑ ● Ⓓ
34. Ⓕ ● Ⓗ Ⓙ
35. Ⓐ Ⓑ ● Ⓓ
36. Ⓕ ● Ⓗ Ⓙ
37. ● Ⓑ Ⓒ Ⓓ
38. Ⓕ Ⓖ ● Ⓙ
39. Ⓐ Ⓑ Ⓒ ●
40. Ⓕ ● Ⓗ Ⓙ
41. Ⓐ Ⓑ ● Ⓓ
42. Ⓕ Ⓖ Ⓗ ●

Test-Taking Strategies Guide

State tests vary widely. Many state tests include items that:

- Use specific **language** to suggest how the problem can best be solved (starting on page 9);

- Require an understanding of different methods (**processes**) to solve problems (starting on page 19);

- Require an understanding and use of different representations (**figures**) of problem situations and answer choices (starting on page 27).

The following pages will provide tips, strategies, and practice items to help you learn how to navigate the state test.

Grade 4 Math Vocabulary List

The following lists include words, phrases, and concepts that students should be familiar with before taking the state test for grade 4 mathematics.

Visualizing, understanding, and applying measurement
- Area
- Capacity
- Diameter
- Height
- Length
- Perimeter
- Radius
- Volume
- Width

Identifying, comparing, defining, and measuring angles
- Acute
- Obtuse
- Right

Identifying, comparing, and drawing shapes
- Circle
- Cube
- Hexagon
- Octagon
- Parallelogram
- Pentagon
- Polygon
- Rectangle
- Rectangular prism
- Square
- Triangle (equilateral, isosceles, right)
- Quadrilateral

Understanding and applying algebraic, geometric, and statistical concepts
- Average (mean)
- Axis, axes
- Bar graph

- Circle graph (pie chart)
- Data
- Edge
- Equivalent fractions
- Face
- Estimating
- Expression
- Factor
- Formula
- Geometric figures
- Greatest common factor (GCF)
- Guess-and-check method
- Least common denominator (LCD), least common multiple (LCM)
- Line graph
- Line segment
- Mean
- Median
- Mode
- Mixed number
- Multiples
- Number line
- Order of operations
- Percent
- Probability
- Range
- Rate
- Ratio
- Sequence
- Table, graph, chart, list (data)
- Transformations (translation, rotation, reflection)
- Vertex
- Whole number

Understanding the Language of the Test

Sometimes paying attention to specific words used in test questions can help you narrow the possible choices before looking at figures or performing calculations.

Spotting these words quickly and knowing what they mean can save you from spending too much time or effort on one question.

Read and compare how each word or phrase in the list below is used in the following examples.

These words or phrases are underlined in the examples but these words will not be underlined on the test.

- Best
- Reasonable
- True
- Exactly
- Appears
- Represents
- Nearest
- Always true
- About

Best (Example 1) ▶

When you see the word <u>best</u> in a test item, some of the choices may be close to the correct answer. However, one choice is better than the rest because it completely or more accurately answers the question. If you see the phrases "best describes," "best represents," "best way," or "best estimate," it's asking you to choose the most accurate.

Strategy *Cross out any choices that have wrong information. Compare the choices that are left to see which one best answers the question.*

Solution:

1. Estimate to find the answer.
2. Round 448 to 450 and 396 to 400.
3. Use the rounded numbers to calculate.

$$450 - 400 = 50$$

Choice D is the best estimate.

Example 1

The table below shows the distances in meters that 4 Olympic swimmers swam in one week.

Olympic Swimmer	Distance in Meters
Carlos	396
Barbara	246
Ricardo	378
Dina	448

Which is the <u>best</u> estimate of how many more meters Dina swam than Carlos?

A 100 meters

B 200 meters

C 75 meters

D 50 meters

Independent Strategy Practice
(Best)

1 Which expression shows the best way to estimate the perimeter of a square that has a side length of 346 centimeters?

    A 400×4

    B 300×4

    C 375×4

    D 350×4

2 The table below shows the total inches of rain during different months of the year.

Month	Amount of Rain (Inches)
January	8
March	14
April	17
July	4
October	7

Which statement best describes the data shown in the table?

    F There was more rain in March than the other months.

    G October had the least amount of rain.

    H It rained the most in the month of April and the least in the month of July.

    J July and October had the same amount of rain.

3 Tessa and Brett were playing a game. For every number that Tessa said, Brett used a rule to name a new number.

Tessa	Brett
7	11
14	18
21	25
28	32

Which statement best describes the rule that Brett used?

    A Add 4.

    B Multiply by 4.

    C Divide by 4.

    D Subtract 4.

4 Esteban arranged some tiles in the pattern shown below.

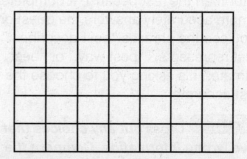

Which number sentence best represents the way Esteban's tiles were arranged?

    F $5 + 7 = 12$

    G $7 \times 5 = 35$

    H $5 \div 7 = 35$

    J $5 \times 6 = 30$

Understanding the Language of the Test

Exactly (Example 2) ▶

When you see <u>exactly</u> in a problem, you are being asked to find a precise answer. Do not estimate. There should only be one correct answer.

Strategy *Choose the necessary operation and then carefully solve the problem to find the exact match.*

Solution: Add to solve.

$$\begin{array}{r} 56 \\ +\ 9 \\ \hline 65 \end{array}$$

After adding 56 + 9, you find that Issandra is exactly 9 inches taller than Amelia. Choice C is the only correct choice.

Nearest (Example 3) ▶

When you see the word <u>nearest</u>, it means to find the closest value. Sometimes you will need to estimate to find the answer.

Strategy *Round numbers before you solve. Then decide which operation to use to solve the problem.*

Solution:

1. Be sure to use the centimeter side of the ruler to measure the rectangle. The length is about 6.8 cm and the width is about 5.5 cm.

2. Round each number to the nearest centimeter.

   6.8 cm ⟶ 7 cm   5.5 cm ⟶ 6 cm

3. Then add to find the perimeter.
   6 + 6 + 7 + 7 = 26 centimeters

Choice B is the correct answer.

Example 2

Amelia is 56 inches tall. Which student is exactly 9 inches taller than Amelia?

Student Name	Height in Inches
Carina	58
Kevin	62
Issandra	65
Jose	71

A Jose   C Issandra

B Carina   D Kevin

Example 3

Daniel drew a rectangle. Use the ruler on the Mathematics Chart to measure the dimensions of his rectangle to the <u>nearest</u> centimeter.

What is the perimeter of Daniel's rectangle?

A 13   C 24

B 26   D 18

Independent Strategy Practice
(Exactly, Nearest)

5 Which two shoe types have a total cost of exactly $81.00?

Shoe Type	Cost
Boots	$50.15
Sandals	$15.25
Sneakers	$30.85
Loafers	$42.50
Tennis Shoes	$38.30

A Boots and Sneakers

B Sandals and Boots

C Loafers and Sandals

D Tennis Shoes and Boots

6 Lucinda buys a measuring tape for $11.35 and a wrench for $6.40. Exactly how much change should she receive if she pays with a twenty-dollar bill?

F $17.75

G $2.25

H $2.00

J $3.00

7 Clarissa has $15.43 in her pocket. To the nearest dollar, which is the best estimate of how much money Clarissa has in her pocket?

A $16.00

B $15.50

C $15.00

D $20.00

8 Samir lives about 1 mile from school. A mile is 5280 feet. To the nearest hundred feet, which is the best estimate of the distance Samir lives from school?

F 5000 ft

G 5250 ft

H 6000 ft

J 5300 ft

Understanding the Language of the Test

Reasonable (Example 4) ▶

When you see the word <u>reasonable</u>, you should look for the choice that makes the most sense or the choice that is closest to your solution. Because you are not looking for an exact answer, you can estimate your answer.

Strategy *Compare the result of your estimated solution to the answer choices. Find the choice that is the closest match.*

Solution:

1. Estimate to find the answer.
2. Round 18 minutes to 20.
3. Multiply.

   20 minutes × 6 = 120 minutes

Choice B is the reasonable answer.

Example 4

It took Maria 18 minutes to complete one puzzle. Which is a <u>reasonable</u> estimate of the time it took for her to complete 6 puzzles?

A 90 minutes

B 120 minutes

C 200 minutes

D 60 minutes

Discuss: How could you check your estimation?

Appears (Example 5) ▶

If you see the phrase <u>appears to</u> in a problem, you will have to study the picture carefully.

Strategy *Check each answer choice against the picture. Make sure you understand the vocabulary in the question and the answer choices.*

Solution:

1. Remember that perpendicular means to intersect at right angles.
2. The only streets that intersect at right angles are Clinton and Carter. Choice D is the correct answer.

Tip

Cross out answers that are wrong. Then choose from the remaining choices.

Example 5

Which streets <u>appear to</u> be perpendicular to each other?

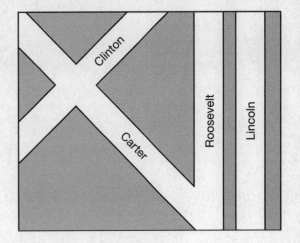

A Lincoln and Roosevelt

B Clinton and Lincoln

C Roosevelt and Carter

D Clinton and Carter

Independent Strategy Practice
(Reasonable, Appears)

9 Mark and Yolanda are playing games. It takes them about 25 minutes to finish each game. They take a 5 minute break between games. What is a reasonable number of games they could play in two hours?

A   150 games

B   12 games

C   4 games

D   7 games

10 Which angle appears to be a right angle?

F   H

G   J

11 Which of the following appears to be an equilateral triangle?

A   C

B   D

12 Which is a reasonable weight for a cat?

F   250 pounds

G   40 ounces

H   10 pounds

J   1,000 pounds

Understanding the Language of the Test

Always true (Example 6) ▶

The phrase <u>always true</u> means that some of the answer choices may be true some of the time, but only one choice is true all of the time.

Strategy *Read each choice and ask yourself, "Is this completely true, all of the time?"*

Solution:

1. Choice A is true sometimes, but only if the parallelogram is also a rectangle.

2. Choice B is never true, since at least two sets of angles are always equal because the sides will always be parallel.

3. Choice C is false, since four sets equals eight sides.

4. Choice D is <u>always true</u>.

Example 6

Which statement is <u>always true</u> about a parallelogram?

A All four angles have the same measure.

B All four angles have different measures.

C There are four sets of parallel sides.

D There are two sets of parallel sides.

True (Example 7) ▶

The word <u>true</u> is not used the same way as the phrase "always true." When you see the word *true* by itself, only one choice is correct. The other choices are false.

Strategy *Cross out the choices that you know are false. If necessary, find an exact solution.*

Solution:

1. Cross out A because $6 \div 2$ does not equal 4.

2. Cross out B because $21 \div 6$ does not equal 7.

3. Cross out D because $30 \div 6 = 6$ is false.

4. The only true choice is C.

Discuss: What numbers would you use to make the other equations true?

Example 7

In which number sentence does 6 make the equation <u>true</u>?

A $\square \div 2 = 4$

B $21 \div \square = 7$

C $24 \div \square = 4$

D $30 \div \square = 6$

Independent Strategy Practice
(Always true, True)

13 Which of the following statements is always true?

    A   A square has 4 right angles.

    B   A square has 4 acute angles.

    C   A square has 2 right angles and 2 obtuse angles.

    D   All angles in a square are greater than 90 degrees.

14 Which statement is always true about a prime number?

    F   It has 2 or more factors.

    G   It is an even number.

    H   It only has 2 factors, the number 1 and itself.

    J   It is sometimes a composite number.

15 Liliana uses a spinner divided into four equal parts numbered from 1 to 4. Which statement is true?

    A   Liliana has $\frac{1}{2}$ of a chance of spinning a 2.

    B   Liliana has $\frac{1}{4}$ of a chance of spinning an even number.

    C   Liliana has $\frac{3}{4}$ of a chance of spinning an odd number.

    D   Liliana has 50% of a chance of spinning an even number.

16 Which statement is true about a cube?

    F   It has exactly 6 edges.

    G   It has exactly 6 faces.

    H   It has exactly 8 edges.

    J   It has exactly 4 vertices.

Understanding the Language of the Test

Represents (Example 8) ▶

The word <u>represent</u> means "to stand for" or "act in place of" something. When you see represent in a problem, it is asking you to match the question with the correct answer choice.

Solution:

1. In Example 8, the sum of Levon's age plus 2 equals Tanisha's age.

$$14 + 2 = 16$$

2. Marcus is half as old as Tanisha so his age can be found by dividing $(14 + 2)$ by 2.

$$(14 + 2) \div 2 = m.$$

Choice C is correct.

Example 8

Levon is 14 years old. His sister Tanisha is 2 years older than Levon, and their brother Marcus is half as old as Tanisha. Which number sentence <u>represents</u> m, Marcus's age?

A $14 \times 2 = m$

B $(14 + 2) \times 2 = m$

C $(14 + 2) \div 2 = m$

D $8 \times 2 \times 2 = m$

About (Example 9) ▶

The word <u>about</u> means "near" or "close to." In some cases, you can estimate to find the answer.

Strategy *There may be more than one way that you can estimate to find the answer. Solve the problem using rounded or compatible numbers. Then look for the answer choice that matches the estimate.*

Solution:

1. We can estimate using compatible numbers.

2. Since 150 is compatible with 10, we round 9 to 10.

3. Then divide using the compatible numbers.

$$150 \div 10 = 15$$

Choice C is correct.

Example 9

Pablo reads 9 pages a day. His book has 150 pages. About how many days will it take him to read the whole book?

A 19

B 25

C 15

D 8

Independent Strategy Practice
(Represents, About)

17 Which number represents point *K* on the number line?

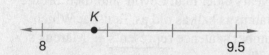

- **A** 8.8
- **B** 9.1
- **C** 8.6
- **D** 8.4

18 Which of the following fractions represents the picture?

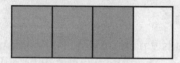

- **F** $\frac{4}{3}$
- **G** $\frac{1}{4}$
- **H** $\frac{3}{5}$
- **J** $\frac{3}{4}$

19 Kenneth began working on his art project at 3:49 P.M. He stopped at 8:10 P.M. About how many hours did he spend working on his art project?

- **A** 4 hours
- **B** 18 hours
- **C** 15 hours
- **D** 6 hours

20 Carolina's basketball practice lasts about 2 hours. She practices one out of every 3 days. About how many hours will she have practiced in 25 days?

- **F** 21
- **G** 16
- **H** 40
- **J** 8

Understanding Process Problems on the Test

The TAKS includes questions that require you to identify the method you would use to solve a given problem, match an equation to a problem situation, identify information needed to solve a problem, or describe relationships between paired numbers. In process problems, you are not usually asked to calculate a solution.

Find the method used (Example 10) ▶

Sometimes you will be asked to describe the steps you would use to solve the problem. This type of problem does not require a calculated answer. Instead, you may have to find one or more steps in a problem-solving method.

When more than one step is used, the steps will need to be shown in the correct order.

Example 10

Edmond and Abram can buy 4 basketball tokens for $1. Each game will cost 2 tokens. Which is a correct way to find the number of games they can play with $24 in tokens?

A Add 4 and 24, and then divide the sum by 2.

B Add 4 and 24, and then multiply the sum by 2.

C Multiply 4 by 24, and then divide the product by 2.

D Multiply 4 by 24, and then multiply the product by 2.

Workspace: Example 10

What information is given and what do we already know?

- 4 tokens cost $1.
- Each game costs 2 tokens.
- They have $24 in tokens.

What are we asked to find or do?

We are asked to find how many games they can play.

How do we solve the problem?

We need to break this problem into steps. First, we will find how many basketball tokens Edmond and Abram have, and then we will find how many games they can play.

Since 4 tokens cost $1, we can multiply 4 by 24 to find the number of tokens they have. We know each game costs 2 tokens. We will divide the number of tokens they have, (4 × 24), by 2. We can use these steps to find how many games they can play.

Compare that step with the answer choices. Is there a clear match?

Yes. Our answer is choice C.

Independent Strategy Practice
(Find the method used)

21 Tiffany had 60 ounces of lemonade in a container. After she poured an equal amount of juice into each of 8 glasses, there were 20 ounces of juice left in the container. What should Tiffany do to find how many ounces of juice she poured into each glass?

A Divide 20 by 8, and then subtract the quotient from 60.

B Subtract 20 from 60, and then divide the difference by 8.

C Add 20 and 8, and then subtract the sum from 60.

D Divide 60 by 8, and then subtract the quotient from 20.

22 Jamel is a 4th grade student. He set a goal to read $2\frac{1}{2}$ hours during a five-day period for an after-school reading program. Jamel recorded how much time he read each day.

Weekday	Reading Time
M	30 minutes
T	30 minutes
W	35 minutes
Th	35 minutes
F	25 minutes

Which method can he use to find whether he met his goal?

F Round the minutes to hours and then add.

G Divide 5 by 30, and then compare the minutes to the $2\frac{1}{2}$ hours.

H Find the total minutes read to see if it is equal to or more than $2\frac{1}{2}$ hours.

J Multiply 5 by the total minutes.

23 Carlota made 2 pounds and 4 ounces of applesauce. Which is the best way to find the total number of ounces of applesauce that Carlota made?

A Multiply 2 by 16, and then add 4.

B Add 2 and 4, and then multiply by 9.

C Multiply 2 and 4, and then divide by 4.

D Multiply 2 by 16, and then add 16.

24 A class has 9 days left to complete 80 squares for a quilt. They have already completed 44 squares. Which method could they use to find the number of squares they must complete each day to finish the squares on time?

F Multiply 44 by 9, and then subtract 80.

G Subtract 44 from 80, and then divide by 9.

H Divide 80 by 9, and then subtract 44.

J Subtract 44 from 80, and then multiply by 9 to find the difference.

Understanding Process Problems on the Test

Matching an equation to a problem situation (Example 11) ▶

Sometimes you will have to match an equation to a given problem situation.

Strategy *Find the specific information in the problem. Use each piece of information to write an equation or a number sentence. Use variables to represent any unknown data.*

Example 11

Beatriz and Hakim were counting the number of people in a community swimming pool. Hakim counted 28 people, and Beatriz counted 5 fewer people than Hakim. Which number sentence could be used to find b, Beatriz's number count?

A $28 \times 5 = b$

B $28 + 5 = b$

C $28 - 5 = b$

D $28 \div 5 = b$

Workspace: Example 11

What information do we know from the problem?

- b = Beatriz's number count
- Hakim's number count = 28
- b = 5 fewer than Hakim's number count

How do we use this information to solve the problem?

We write a number sentence using the information we are given.

$$28 - 5 = b$$

Compare your equation to the answer choices. Is there a match?

Yes. Our answer matches choice C.

Independent Strategy Practice
(Matching an equation to a problem situation)

25 Jade and her family have 2 newspapers delivered to their house every day. When they came back from vacation, there were 18 newspapers on their front porch. Which equation could be used to find the number of days (d) Jade and her family were on vacation?

   A $18 - 2 = d$

   B $18 \times 2 = d$

   C $18 \div 2 = d$

   D $18 + 2 = d$

26 Ernesto rides his bike 7 miles each way to school. He goes to school every day Monday through Friday. Which number sentence could you use to find out how many miles (m) Ernesto rides to school in one week?

   F $7 + 2 + 5 = m$

   G $7 \times 5 \div 2 = m$

   H $5 \times 7 + 2 = m$

   J $7 \times 2 \times 5 = m$

27 Daisy bought 3 paintbrushes for $6 each and 4 paint bottles for $5 each. Which number sentence can be used to find the total number of dollars (d) Daisy spent on these supplies?

   A $18 + 20 = d$

   B $9 \times 9 = d$

   C $9 + 9 = d$

   D $18 \times 20 = d$

28 The windows in the library are being replaced. There are 3 large rooms in the library, and each room has 12 windows. Which number sentence could be used to find the total number of windows (w) being replaced in the library?

   F $12 \times 3 = w$

   G $12 \div 3 = w$

   H $3 \times 12 + 3 = w$

   J $12 - 3 = w$

Understanding Process Problems on the Test

Identifying Information Needed (Example 12) ▶

Sometimes you will be asked to determine what information is needed in order to solve a problem. There may be a piece of information missing from the information given, but it is needed to solve the problem.

Strategy *Read the whole problem. Look for what you know and what you need to find. Ask yourself questions to try to find the missing information.*

Sometimes you may also be asked to identify the question that could be answered with the information provided in the problem. For this type of question, you will be asked to choose the question that could be answered with the information given in the problem.

Example 12

Rafael wants to paint a border around the top of the walls in his bedroom. The border has a design that is 18 inches long. He will have to repeat the design several times. What information is needed to find the number of times Rafael will need to repeat the design?

A The height of the walls

B The perimeter of the bedroom

C The amount of paint needed for the border

D The number of minutes needed to paint each design

Workspace: Example 12

What information can we get from the problem?

- *Rafael wants to paint a border around his bedroom.*

- *The border has a design that is 18 inches long.*

- *Rafael will have to repeat the design.*

How do we use this information to solve the problem?

We need to know how many times Rafael will need to repeat the design, but we don't know the distance around the bedroom. The distance around the bedroom is the perimeter.

Which information is missing? Which choice matches our answer?

The perimeter of the bedroom is missing, which is choice B.

Discuss: If the perimeter of the room is 20 feet, how many inches is that? How many times would the pattern repeat?

Tip

Write a separate statement about each piece of information in the problem.

Independent Strategy Practice
(Identifying information needed)

29 Ana is saving to buy a skateboard. She has already saved $5.25. What information is needed to find the amount Ana still needs to save in order to buy the skateboard?

A How Ana will earn the money

B How often Ana is paid

C How much the skateboard costs

D The color and design of the skateboard

30 At a flower shop, roses are sold in bundles. Each bundle costs $12.00. Mr. Ramon needs to buy 48 roses to make table decorations for a banquet. Which question must be answered to find the amount Mr. Ramon will pay for the roses?

F How many people will be at the banquet?

G How many roses are in a bundle?

H How many tables will need decorations?

J How much does one dozen roses costs?

31 Edna needs to swim $2\frac{1}{2}$ miles during practice. She has already swam 4 laps. What information would help Edna find the distance she still needs to swim?

A The depth of the pool

B The shape of the pool

C The temperature of the water

D The length of the pool

32 A fourth grade class is going on a field trip. The teacher has organized 7 equal groups of students. Each group has 4 students. What question could be answered with this given information?

F How many students are going on the field trip?

G Where are the students going for the field trip?

H How much is the cost of a museum ticket?

J How much time will the students spend at the museum?

Understanding Process Problems on the Test

Describing the relationship between paired numbers (Example 13) ▶

Sometimes you will be asked to find the relationship between numbers in a table.

Strategy *Find the possible relationships between the first pair of numbers. Check those possible relationships to see which apply to the other pairs of numbers.*

Tip

Sometimes the word <u>pattern</u> will be used instead of relationship.

Example 13

The following table shows the number of United States Senators per state.

Senators Per State

Number of States	6	10	18	27
Total Number of Senators	12	20	36	54

What is the relationship between the number of states and the total number of senators?

A The number of states is 5 more than the total number of senators.

B The number of states is 6 times the total number of senators.

C The total number of senators is 10 more than the number of states.

D The total number of senators is 2 times the number of states.

Workspace: Example 13

What are the possible relationships between the first pair of numbers?

$$6 + 6 = 12 \text{ or } 6 \times 2 = 12$$

- We know that $6 \times 2 = 12$ is the inverse operation of $12 \div 2 = 6$ and that $6 + 6 = 12$ is the inverse operation of $12 - 6 = 6$, so we only need to try the first two relationships.

- There are not any other possible relationships between the first pair of numbers.

Check the first possible relationship against the next pair of numbers.

- Since $10 + 5$ does not equal 20, we know that adding 5 is *not* the correct relationship.

- Since 10×2 *does* equal 20, we multiply both 18 and 27 by 2.

- Since $18 \times 2 = 36$ and $27 \times 2 = 54$, so we know that *multiply by* 2 is the correct relationship.

Tip

Check the possible relationships against the answer choices. If only one of the possible relationships is also an answer choice, then that relationship is the correct answer.

Independent Strategy Practice
(Describing the relationship between paired numbers)

33 The table below shows the number of cubes and the number of faces on those cubes.

Number of Cubes	Number of Faces
3	18
6	36
9	54

What is the relationship between the number of cubes and the total number of faces?

A   Number of cubes $\times$ 4 = number of faces

B   Number of cubes + 15 = number of faces

C   Number of cubes $\times$ 6 = number of faces

D   Number of cubes + 30 = number of faces

34 Payton rides his bike to and from school every day. The table shows the total number of miles he rode after different numbers of days.

Number of Days	Total Number of Miles
4	28
6	42
8	56

If this pattern continues, how many miles will Payton ride in 12 days?

F   80

G   63

H   77

J   84

35 The table below shows the number of puzzles that Yasmin puts together versus the number of puzzles her little brother Rashid puts together.

Number of Puzzles Completed

Yasmin	5	10	15	25
Rashid	15	30	45	75

What is the relationship between the number of puzzles Yasmin completes and the number of puzzles Rashid completes?

A   The number of puzzles Rashid completes is 3 times that of Yasmin.

B   The number of puzzles Yasmin completes is 3 times that of Rashid.

C   The number of puzzles Yasmin completes is 10 less than Rashid.

D   The number of puzzles Rashid completes is 10 more than Yasmin.

36 The table below shows the relationship between inches and feet.

Inches	2	4	5	7
Feet	24	48	60	84

If this pattern continues, how many inches will be in 10 feet?

F   132 inches

G   96 inches

H   120 inches

J   108 inches

Understanding the Figures of the Test

State tests use different kinds of figures, such as models, tables, graphs, geometric figures, and number lines.

Many of the questions on the test may contain figures. The figures are there to help you solve the problem.

When you start a test item that contains a figure of any kind:

- First, read the question and all of the answer choices.

- Then study the figure carefully for information that can be used to solve the problem.

- Solve the problem. Then use the figure to check your answer.

Try to solve the example problems below using the same method.

Identifying fractions and equivalent fractions using models (Example 14) ▶

Some questions may show a model shaded to represent a fraction. Then you will choose another model that shows an equivalent fraction.

Strategy *Name the fraction for each model. Find the answer choice that is equivalent to the fraction shown in the problem.*

Solution:

1. Look at the amount of shaded area in each answer choice.

2. In the model, $\frac{6}{8}$ is shaded. Choices B and D have shading similar to the model. Write the fraction for each choice.

$$B = \frac{5}{8} \qquad D = \frac{3}{4}$$

3. We know that $\frac{5}{8}$ is not equivalent to $\frac{6}{8}$. We see that $\frac{3}{4}$ is equivalent to $\frac{6}{8}$. Choice D is correct.

Tip

Equivalent fractions will have the same amount of shaded area.

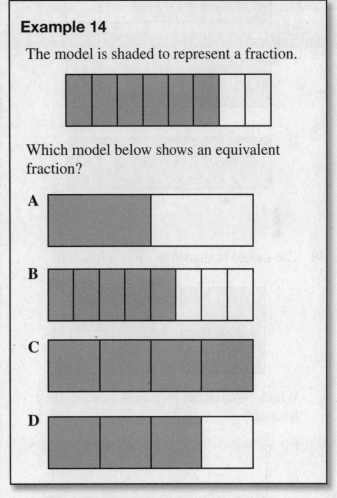

Example 14

The model is shaded to represent a fraction.

Which model below shows an equivalent fraction?

A

B

C

D

Discuss: What fraction of choice A is shaded? Choice C?

Independent Strategy Practice
(Identifying fractions and equivalent fractions using models)

37 The model is shaded to show a fraction.

Which model below shows an equivalent fraction?

A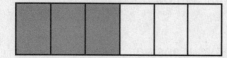

B

C

D

38 The model is shaded to show a fraction.

Which fraction below names an equivalent fraction?

F $\dfrac{7}{4}$

G $\dfrac{4}{7}$

H $\dfrac{5}{4}$

J $\dfrac{1}{4}$

39 The model is shaded to show a fraction.

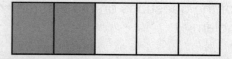

Which model below shows an equivalent fraction?

A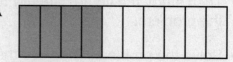

B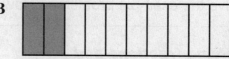

C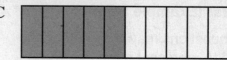

D

40 The model is shaded to represent a fraction.

Which fraction below names an equivalent fraction?

F $\dfrac{9}{11}$

G $\dfrac{10}{9}$

H $\dfrac{11}{3}$

J $\dfrac{10}{3}$

Understanding the Figures of the Test

Relating fractions to decimals using models (Example 15) ▶

Models can help relate fractions and mixed numbers to decimals.

Strategy *Think of the mixed number as two parts—a whole number and a fraction.*

Solution:

1. The fraction $3\frac{56}{100}$ is read as "three and fifty-six hundredths."

2. The whole-number part will be to the left of the decimal point.

    $$3.\_\_$$

3. The fraction part will be the decimal part. The denominator is indicated in the decimal number by the number of places to the right of the decimal point.

    $$3.56$$

Choice C is correct.

Discuss: How can you use the models shown to check your answer?

Comparing fractions using models (Example 16) ▶

Some questions may ask you to compare fractions using models. Remember that the shaded parts represent the numerators.

Strategy *Name each fraction shown by the models. Reduce each fraction if necessary. Look at the amount of space shaded in each model. Use the fractions and a comparison symbol to write a statement describing the shaded amounts shown.*

Choice C is correct.

Tip

If the shaded parts are different sizes, cross out answers that have equal signs. If the shaded parts are the same size, cross out answers with greater than or less than symbols.

Example 15

This model is shaded to represent $3\frac{56}{100}$.

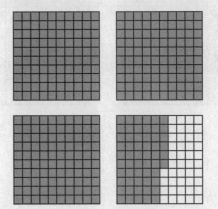

What decimal does the model represent?

A 356.0

B .356

C 3.56

D 35.6

Example 16

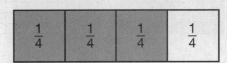

The models above are shaded to show that:

A $\frac{3}{4} = \frac{3}{5}$

B $\frac{1}{4} < \frac{1}{5}$

C $\frac{3}{4} > \frac{3}{5}$

D $\frac{3}{4} < \frac{3}{5}$

Independent Strategy Practice
(Relating fractions to decimals using models)

41 The model is shaded to represent $1\frac{7}{10}$.

 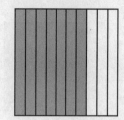

Which decimal does the model represent?

A 1.7

B 0.17

C 17.0

D 10.7

42 The model is shaded to represent $1\frac{33}{100}$.

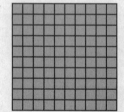 

What decimal does the model represent?

F 133.0

G 13.3

H 1.33

J 0.133

43

| $\frac{1}{4}$ | $\frac{1}{4}$ | $\frac{1}{4}$ | $\frac{1}{4}$ |

| $\frac{1}{3}$ | $\frac{1}{3}$ | $\frac{1}{3}$ |

The models above are shaded to show that:

A $\frac{1}{4} = \frac{1}{3}$

B $\frac{2}{4} > \frac{1}{3}$

C $\frac{1}{3} < \frac{1}{4}$

D $\frac{1}{3} > \frac{1}{4}$

44 The models below are shaded to show that:

F $\frac{3}{4} = \frac{5}{8}$

G $\frac{2}{6} > \frac{1}{4}$

H $\frac{3}{4} < \frac{5}{8}$

J $\frac{3}{4} > \frac{5}{8}$

Understanding the Figures of the Test

Analyzing data from a table (Example 17) ▶

Sometimes you will be asked to make decisions based on information found in tables.

Strategy *Before looking at the table, read the entire question carefully. Then look at the table and find the information needed to solve the problem. It may take more than one step to solve the problem.*

Solution:

1. Add the cost of the items we know they bought.

   $3.49 + $2.99 + $1.99 = $8.47

2. Since they had $10.00, we subtract to find out how much they had left.

   $10.00 − $8.47 = $1.53

3. The only item that costs less than $1.53 is honey. The answer is choice B.

Discuss: How could this problem be simplified by rounding?

Example 17

The prices of food items are shown below in the table.

Item	Price
Bread	$3.49
Orange Juice	$2.99
Grapes	$3.99
Honey	$1.49
Peanut Butter	$1.99
Turkey	$4.49
Cheese	$4.49

Jenny and Sun had $10.00. They bought bread, orange juice, and peanut butter. They had money left over for one more item. Which item could they buy?

A Grapes   C Turkey

B Honey   D Cheese

Analyzing data from a table (continued) (Example 18) ▶

Sometimes you will be given a table with missing data. You will be asked to use the information given to find the missing data.

Strategy *Read the question carefully. Use the information given to write a number sentence to find the missing data.*

Solution:

1. 20 + 40 + 80 + ☐ = 160
2. 140 + ☐ = 160
3. ☐ = 160 − 140
4. ☐ = 20 fish

Choice A is correct.

Example 18

The table below shows the number of animals Ervin saw on his camping trip.

Animal	Number of Sightings
Lizard	20
Squirrel	40
Earthworm	80
Fish	

Ervin saw a total of 160 animals. Which of the following could be the number of fish he saw?

A 20   C 40

B 30   D 10

Independent Strategy Practice
(Analyzing data from a table)

45 A store had a sale on camping equipment. The sale prices are shown in the table below.

Camping Equipment

Item	Price
Tent	99.99
Sleeping Bag	39.95
Canteen	21.99
Flashlight	9.99
Sunscreen	4.99
Mosquito Net	12.99
Stove	29.99

Billy and his father had $170.00. They bought a tent, a sleeping bag, and a canteen. They had enough money left over to buy one more item. Which item could they buy?

A Flashlight   **C** Sunscreen

B Mosquito Net   **D** Stove

46 Four friends saved up money from working part-time jobs to buy tickets to the football game. The table below shows the amount of money saved by each friend.

Money Saved

Friend	Amount of Money
Jonah	$16
Clive	$11
Terry	$21
Michael	$10

After putting their money together, the friends bought 4 tickets that cost $13 each. Which shows the amount of money they had left?

F $6   **H** $8

G $10   **J** $13

47 The table below shows the total number of miles Alison and Daniel rode on their bicycle trip.

Number of Days	Total Number of Miles
1	11
2	14
3	19
4	

Alison and Daniel rode a total of 60 miles. Which of the following could be the number of miles they rode on day 4 of the bicycle trip?

A 60   **C** 20

B 12   **D** 16

48 The table below shows the number of stamps collected by five stamp collectors in the school stamp club.

Stamps Collected

Stamp Collector	Stamps Collected
Michelle	27
Pierre	76
Ariana	61
Bethany	40
Karl	

The stamp club collected a total of 240 stamps. Which of the following could be the number of stamps Karl collected?

F 26   **H** 34

G 40   **J** 36

Understanding the Figures of the Test

Interpreting bar graphs (Example 19) ▶

Sometimes you will be asked to make decisions about information presented in bar graphs. Bar graphs can be written vertically (up and down) or horizontally (sideways).

Strategy *Read the entire question carefully before studying the graph. Look at the labels on the graph. Decide what information you will need from the graph to solve the problem.*

Solution:

1. Find the bar marked "Dimitri" and follow it up and to the left. Dimitri scored a total of 24 points.

2. Since he scored the same number of points in each game, we can divide 24 by 3 to find the answer.

   $$24 \div 3 = 8$$

Choice D is correct.

Discuss: Altogether, how many points did Jack and Janisha average over the three games?

Interpreting bar graphs (continued) (Example 20) ▶

This is a horizontal bar graph (it runs sideways). Notice that the bar for Motorcycles stops halfway between 6 and 8. This means that its value is 7.

Strategy *Read the entire question carefully before studying the graph. Make sure you know what information you need from the graph and what steps you will need to perform.*

Solution:

1. Add the number of trucks and vans.

   $$12 + 10 = 22$$

2. Subtract the number of motorcylces from the sum of the trucks and vans.

   $$22 - 7 = 15$$

3. The answer is choice D.

Example 19

The graph below shows the total number of points each player scored over three games in a ping-pong tournament.

If Dimitri scored the same number of points in all three games, how many points did he score in the first game?

A 24   C 12

B 16   D 8

Example 20

The graph below shows the number of vehicles that Stan counted in the mall parking lot.

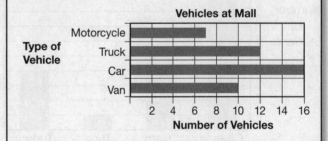

According to the graph, how many more Trucks and Vans were counted than Motorcycles?

A 22   C 14

B 25   D 15

Independent Strategy Practice
(Interpreting bar graphs)

49 The graph below shows the total number of hours that Thurston worked over four weeks.

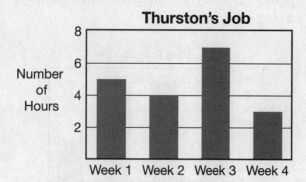

If Thurston earned $7 an hour, how much money did he earn during Week 3?

A $28

B $49

C $35

D $21

50 The graph below shows how many students ate each kind of sandwich for lunch on Thursday.

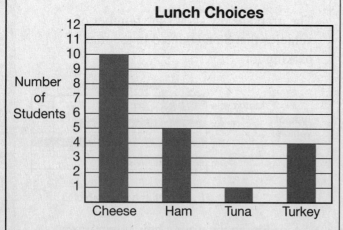

How many more students ate a cheese sandwich than ate a tuna sandwich?

F 1   **H** 9

G 5   **J** 11

51 The graph below shows the number of students in each fourth-grade class at Jackson's school.

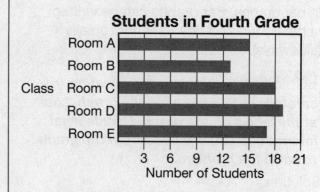

Which 2 rooms have a combined total of 34 students?

A Rooms D and A

B Rooms E and B

C Rooms C and A

D Rooms E and C

52 The graph below shows the number of birds counted by students in Mr. Davari's science class during a field trip to the park.

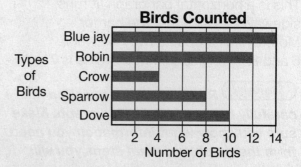

According to the graph, how many more sparrows and robins were counted than blue jays?

F 6   **H** 14

G 8   **J** 20

Understanding the Figures of the Test

Identifying geometric figures (Example 21) ▶

Sometimes you will be asked to identify types of angles. Remember that there are three types of angles:

Acute (less than 90°)

Right (90°)

Obtuse (more than 90°)

In Example **21**, angles 1 and 3 are acute angles because they are both smaller than a right angle. Choice C is correct.

Identifying geometric figures (continued) (Example 22) ▶

Sometimes you will be asked to identify types of lines.

Perpendicular:

Parallel:

In Example **22**, line *M* is perpendicular to line *L*. Choice A is correct.

Tip

Parallel lines never intersect and are the same distance apart at every point. Perpendicular lines intersect and form right angles.

Example 21

In the figure below, which two angles appear to be acute?

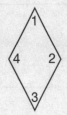

A Angles 1 and 2

B Angles 3 and 4

C Angles 1 and 3

D Angles 2 and 4

Example 22

Which line is perpendicular to line *L*?

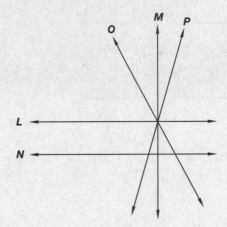

A Line *M*

B Line *N*

C Line *O*

D Line *P*

Independent Strategy Practice
(Identifying geometric figures)

53 Which of the four angles in this figure is an acute angle?

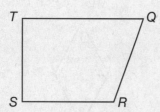

- **A** angle *T*
- **B** angle *Q*
- **C** angle *R*
- **D** angle *S*

54 Which of the following figures has four right angles?

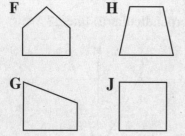

55 Which of the following figures are parallel to each other?

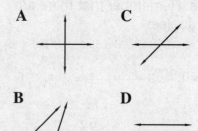

56 Which of the following figures are perpendicular?

Understanding the Figures of the Test

Describing geometric figures (Example 23) ▶

Sometimes you will be asked to describe geometric figures. Two-dimensional shapes can be described by the number of sides and angles they have.

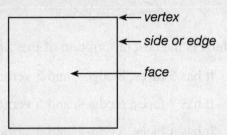

All three shapes have six or more sides. Choice C is correct.

Discuss: Why are all three figures considered polygons? What are the polygon names for the last two figures?

Describing geometric figures (continued) (Example 24) ▶

Sometimes you will be asked to describe solids or three-dimensional figures. Solids have *sides* (or *edges*), *vertices*, and *faces*. You may be asked to describe or identify the figure using the edges, vertices, and faces.

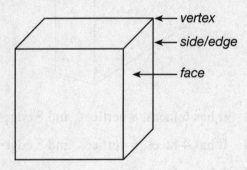

The square pyramid has 5 vertices. Choice B is correct.

Example 23

Dove drew the following shapes:

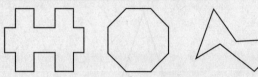

Which statement best describes the shapes Dove drew?

A closed figures with 9 vertices

B closed figures with 5 sides

C closed figures with 6 or more sides

D closed figures with 2 faces

Example 24

How many vertices does this square pyramid have?

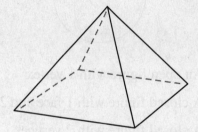

A 8

B 5

C 4

D 9

Independent Strategy Practice
(Describing geometric figures)

57 Which is the best description of the following shape?

A A closed figure with 2 faces

B A closed figure with 3 vertices

C A closed figure with 2 edges

D A closed figure with 1 face and 2 edges

58 Paulina drew a circle. Which is the best description of a circle?

F An open figure with 1 vertex

G A closed figure with 1 face and 2 edges

H A closed figure with 2 vertices

J A closed figure with 1 face and no edges

59 The figure below is the same shape as several Egyptian landmarks. It is a pyramid.

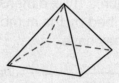

Which is the best description of this figure?

A It has 5 faces, 8 edges, and 5 vertices.

B It has 3 faces, 6 edges, and 5 vertices.

C It has 4 faces, 8 edges, and 3 vertices.

D It has 3 faces, 6 edges, and 6 vertices.

60 Which is the best description of a cereal box?

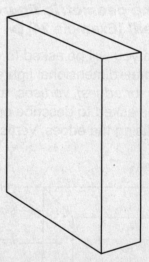

F It has 6 faces, 8 vertices, and 8 edges.

G It has 4 faces, 6 vertices, and 8 edges.

H It has 6 faces, 8 vertices, and 12 edges.

J It has 4 faces, 8 vertices, and 12 edges.

Understanding the Figures of the Test

Naming points on a number line (Example 25) ▶

Sometimes there will be questions about number lines. Be sure you understand what each tick mark on the number line means before answering the question.

Strategy *Read the question carefully. Remember to count the spaces between two whole numbers, not the tick marks. A point on a number line is named by its distance from 0.*

Solution:

The number line has two spaces between whole numbers.

Point P represents $3\frac{1}{2}$. Choice D is correct.

Tip

On some number lines the distance from one tick mark to the next is not 1. You may need to count by twos, by fives, or by some other number.

Example 25

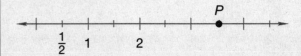

What number on the number line does point P best represent?

A 4

B $2\frac{1}{2}$

C 3

D $3\frac{1}{2}$

Naming points on a number line (continued) (Example 26) ▶

Sometimes the number line will be labled using fractions or decimals. Use the same strategy that you used when the number line was labeled using whole numbers.

Strategy *Read the question carefully. Study the number line and determine what number each tick mark on the number line represents.*

Solution:

1. Count the number of spaces from 2 to 3. There are 10 ten spaces, which means the number line is divided into tenths.

2. Point Q is six tick marks (or six tenths) away from 2.

3. Point Q is located at 2.6. Choice B is correct.

Discuss: How would you write 2.6 as a fraction?

Example 26

What number on the number line does point Q best represent?

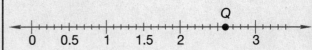

A 2.5

B 2.6

C 2.7

D 2.4

Tip

Use the halfway mark between whole numbers (0.5 or $\frac{1}{2}$) to help count.

Independent Strategy Practice
(Naming points on a number line)

61 To which number on the number line below is the arrow pointing?

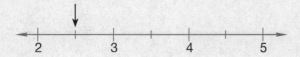

A 4

B $2\frac{1}{2}$

C 3

D $4\frac{1}{2}$

62 Which number on the number line does point *K* represent?

F $5\frac{1}{2}$

G $5\frac{3}{4}$

H $4\frac{1}{2}$

J $5\frac{1}{4}$

63 To which decimal number on the number line below is the arrow pointing?

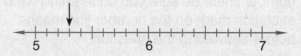

A 6.1

B 5.5

C 5.8

D 6.3

64 Which decimal number on the number line does point *M* represent?

F 10.2

G 9.8

H 10.5

J 10.9

Understanding the Figures of the Test

Transformations ▶

You will sometimes be asked to identify or describe the transformation that moves one figure to the same position of another figure. The pair of figures that show a transformation will always be congruent.

Strategy *Study each pair of figures carefully. Use the words* slide, flip, *or* turn *to describe how one figure can be moved to the same position as the other.*

Tip

Remember that:

- A translation is the same as a *slide*.
- A rotation is the same as a *turn*.
- A reflection is the same as a *flip*.

Solution:

1. Look at each pair of figures.
2. Ask yourself if the figure flips to make a mirror image.
3. Answer choice G is correct.

Discuss: What transformation is shown in each of the other answer choices?

Example 27

Which of the following pair of figures shows only a reflection?

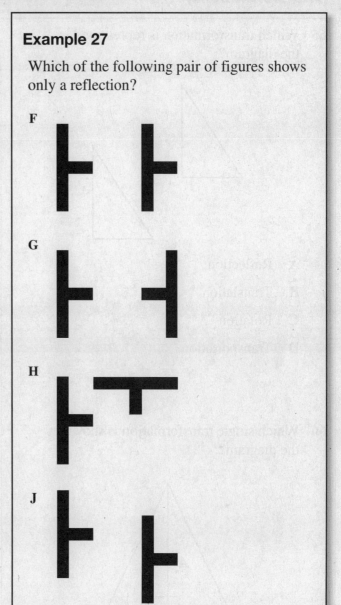

Independent Strategy Practice
(Transformations)

65 Which transformation is represented in the diagram?

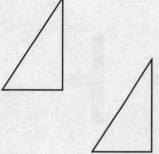

   A   Reflection

   B   Translation

   C   Rotation

   D   Transportation

66 Which single transformation is shown in the diagram?

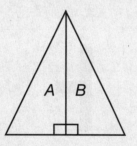

   F   Reflection

   G   Translation

   H   Rotation

   J   Transylvania

67 Which of the following pictures shows only a reflection?

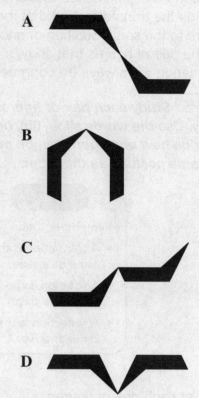

To the Student

Dear Student,

The Practice Test you are about to take is intended to help you prepare for the state mathematics test. The questions are based on math concepts you have learned throughout the school year.

This test will ask you to use your math skills to answer questions and solve problems. The state mathematics test helps teachers, schools, and parents know what you have learned.

Taking the Practice Test should help you be more comfortable when you take the state test because you will already know what it looks like.

Before starting, listen carefully to your teacher's instructions and read all written directions.

As you work through the test, you might find that some questions are harder than others. As on the state test, you should be able to work ahead and still have time to come back to difficult questions you skipped. Put a mark next to any question you did not understand so your teacher can help you after the test.

Remember to continue working until you see the "STOP" sign on the last page.

Do your best!

MATHEMATICS
Practice Test
GRADE 4

Student Tips

- Make sure you have two sharpened No. 2 pencils with erasers before beginning the Practice Test.

- Pay attention to your teacher for instructions.

- Read and follow written directions carefully. Ask your teacher to explain any directions you do not understand.

- You will not be allowed to use a calculator. Be prepared to work out calculations using mental math or paper and pencil.

- You will not be allowed to use scratch paper during the Practice Test. However, you are allowed to write on the Practice Test pages. Use the space provided around each question to solve each problem.

- Read each question and all of the answer choices before studying any figures. Some figures are for illustration only and will not help you solve the problem.

- Write each step you use to answer each problem. Skip and come back to difficult questions later.

- Circle your answer in your test booklet before entering it on your answer document. That way, if you skip a space or lose track of your place, it will be easy to compare your answers and to find the error.

- If you don't know an answer, cross out the answer choices that you know are wrong. Choose the best answer from the choices that remain.

- Drawing a picture may help you understand and solve a problem.

- Check your work so you don't make careless errors.

- Fill in the answer circle completely. Do not make any stray marks on your answer document. If you change an answer, be sure to completely erase the old answer.

- Work until you see the "STOP" sign on the last page of the test.

Grade 4 Mathematics Chart

Length

Metric

1 kilometer	=	1000 meters
1 meter	=	100 centimeters
1 centimeter	=	10 millimeters

Customary

1 mile	=	1760 yards
1 mile	=	5280 feet
1 yard	=	3 feet
1 foot	=	12 inches

Capacity and Volume

Metric	Customary
1 liter = 1000 milliliters	1 gallon = 4 quarts
	1 gallon = 128 ounces
	1 quart = 2 pints
	1 pint = 2 cups
	1 cup = 8 ounces

Mass and Weight

Metric	Customary
1 kilogram = 1000 grams	1 ton = 2000 pounds
1 gram = 1000 milligrams	1 pound = 16 ounces

Time

1 year = 365 days
1 year = 12 months
1 year = 52 weeks
1 week = 7 days
1 day = 24 hours
1 hour = 60 minutes
1 minute = 60 seconds

Formulas

Perimeter	square	$P = 4s$
	rectangle	$P = 2l + 2w$ or $P = 2(l + w)$
Area	rectangle	$A = lw$ or $A = bh$

Centimeters

Inches

Sample Questions

DIRECTIONS

Read each question. Then fill in the correct answer on your answer document. If a correct answer is not here, mark the letter for "Not here."

Sample A

Which digit is in the thousands place in the number 4,861,392?

A 6

B 4

C 1

D Not here

Sample B

Joey has 8 books. Roberto has twice as many books as Joey has. How many books does Roberto have?

Record your answer and fill in the bubbles on your answer document. Be sure to use the correct place value.

⓪	⓪
①	①
②	②
③	③
④	④
⑤	⑤
⑥	⑥
⑦	⑦
⑧	⑧
⑨	⑨

1 Which word below identifies an angle that measures 171°?

A Right

B Obtuse

C Acute

D Straight

2 Which of the following statements about the probability of the letters in the set below is true?

A, M, M, N, G, H, A, M

F The probability of a letter in the set being "A" is 3 out of 8.

G The probability of a letter in the set being "H" is the same as the probability of a letter in the set being "M."

H The probability of a letter in the set being "M" is 3 out of 8.

J The probability of a letter in the set being "N" is 1 out of 7.

3 The table below shows the number of pentagons and the number of sides of these pentagons.

Sides on Pentagons

Number of Pentagons	Number of Sides
3	15
6	30
9	45
12	60

Which is the correct description of the relationship shown in the table?

A Number of pentagons + 15 = number of sides

B Number of pentagons + 24 = number of sides

C Number of pentagons × 6 = number of sides

D Number of pentagons × 5 = number of sides

GO ON

4 John wants to collect 47 rare coins. So far he has collected 15 coins. How many more coins does he need?

    F   32

    G   40

    H   18

    J   62

6 A square has a side length of 12.2 inches. Estimate the perimeter of the square.

    F   24 inches

    G   18 inches

    H   48 inches

    J   144 inches

5 If $111 \times 10 = 1{,}110$, then what is the product of 101×10?

    A   1,101

    B   1,010

    C   1,001

    D   1,100

GO ON

7 What type of triangle is shown below?

A   Right triangle

B   Equilateral triangle

C   Obtuse triangle

D   Scalene triangle

8 The model shows a circle divided into equal parts. Which fraction below represent the shaded part of the model?

F $\dfrac{1}{6}$

G $\dfrac{3}{6}$

H $\dfrac{5}{6}$

J $\dfrac{2}{3}$

GO ON

9 Which rule describes how to find the next term in this number pattern?

$$256, 64, 16, \underline{\hspace{1cm}}, \ldots$$

A   Multiply 16 by 4

B   Divide 16 by 4

C   Subtract 4 from 16

D   Add 4 to 16

10 A gallon of water is 128 ounces of water. A gallon equals 4 quarts. How many ounces equal 3 quarts?

F   96 ounces

G   64 ounces

H   48 ounces

J   32 ounces

11 The bar graph below shows the total goods (in tons) shipped through a Texas waterway for the years 2000 through 2004.

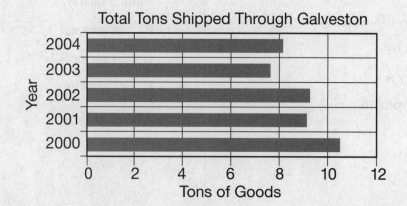

According to the graph, in which year were the fewest tons of goods shipped through Galveston?

A 2001

B 2002

C 2003

D 2004

GO ON

12 Miyu works in an apple orchard. There are 51 apple trees. It took Miyu 37 minutes to pick fresh apples from one tree. Which method can Miyu use to estimate how long it will take, in minutes, to pick fresh apples from all 51 trees?

F Multiply 51 and 37.

G Round, and then multiply 50 and 40.

H Round, and then add 50 and 40.

J Add 51 and 37.

13 In which number sentence does 8 make the equation true?

A $\square \div 2 = 16$

B $40 \div 8 = \square$

C $72 \div \square = 6$

D $56 \div \square = 7$

14 Which is a good description of a pentagon?

F A closed figure with 4 sides and 4 vertices

G An open figure with 8 sides and 4 vertices

H A closed figure with 6 sides and 6 vertices

J A closed figure with 5 sides and 5 vertices

GO ON

15 A rectangular box is half filled using 16 unit cubes. Estimate the total volume of the box.

 A   16 cubic units

 B   40 cubic units

 C   48 cubic units

 D   64 cubic units

16 We can find that 72 is divisible by 9 because the digits add up to 9. Which of the following numbers is also divisible by 9?

 F   171

 G   123

 H   149

 J   143

17 Which array below does **NOT** model factors of 16?

 A

 B

 C

 D

GO ON ▶

18 Isabella has three hundred seventeen songs on her music player. Kenta has five hundred eighty-one songs on his music player. How many more songs does Kenta have compared to Isabella?

F 196 songs

G 264 songs

H 276 songs

J 288 songs

19 Which decimal number does the model represent?

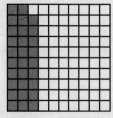

A 0.71

B 0.03

C 0.07

D 0.29

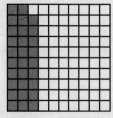
GO ON

20 Which of the following is most likely the next number in Row A?

A	234	345	456	567
B	131	171	181	161

F   191

G   111

H   678

J   876

---

21 Matias used a five-dollar bill to pay for items that cost $3.17 altogether. How much money should Matias get back? Record your answer in the gridded response box on the answer document.

22 Which expression shows how to estimate 257 divided by 6 using compatible numbers?

F $240 \div 6 = 40$

G $252 \div 6 = 42$

H $200 \div 5 = 40$

J $300 \div 6 = 50$

GO ON

23 Which could be the measure of the angle shown below?

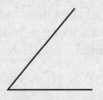

A   25°

B   50°

C   90°

D   110°

24 What is the perimeter of a rectangle that is 15 centimeters long and 4 centimeters wide?

15 cm

4 cm

F   80 centimeters

G   38 centimeters

H   22 centimeters

J   19 centimeters

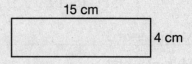

25 Which phrase describes all of the numbers in the counting pattern below?

$$3, 7, 11, 15, 19, \ldots$$

A   Multiples of 3

B   Multiples of 4

C   Factors of 21

D   Odd numbers

26 Rodrigo has six pennies, one nickel, two dimes, and one quarter in his pocket. How can Rodrigo write this money amount using a dollar sign and a decimal point?

F $0.31

G $0.46

H $0.51

J $0.56

27 Ethan has 100 stacks of pennies. There are 10 pennies in each stack. Which number sentence correctly shows how to find how much money Ethan has, and shows the amount written using a dollar sign and decimal point?

A $10 \times 0.10 \times 10 = \$1.00$

B $100 \times 0.01 \times 10 = \$10.00$

C $100 \times 0.10 \times 10 = \$100.00$

D $10 \times 0.01 \times 1.00 = \$0.10$

GO ON ▶

28 The graph below shows the number of club sandwiches ordered at the deli counter.

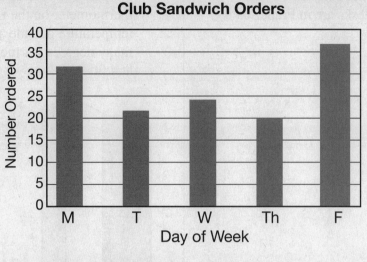

Club Sandwich Orders

According to the graph, which statement appears to be true?

F More club sandwiches were ordered on Monday than on Friday.

G The least number of club sandwiches were ordered on Tuesday.

H About 24 club sandwiches were ordered on Wednesday.

J Club sandwiches were ordered more than 25 times each day.

GO ON

29 Francisca's classroom has twenty-six desks. Jacob's classroom has sixty-two desks. How many fewer desks are in Francisca's classroom?

A 34

B 36

C 44

D 46

30 The thermometer on the left shows the temperature outside at 9:00 A.M. The thermometer on the right shows the temperature outside at 4:30 P.M. How many degrees warmer was the temperature at 4:30 P.M.?

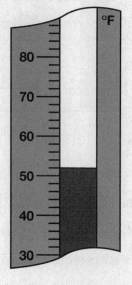 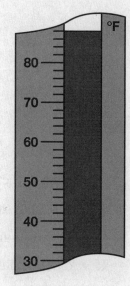

F 32 degrees

G 34 degrees

H 35 degrees

J 36 degrees

GO ON

31 Which expression shows the addition problem below as a multiplication problem?

$$8 + 8 + 8 + 8 + 8 + 8$$

A 8×8

B 8×7

C 8×6

D 8×5

32 Fabio wants to buy three items at the grocery store that are priced at $5.61 each. If Fabio rounds the price to the nearest dollar to estimate the total cost, about how much will Fabio spend to buy all three items?

F $18.00

G $16.83

H $16.80

J $15.00

GO ON

33 In the picture below, there are 3 nickels, 2 dimes, and one quarter. What is the probability that a coin chosen from the set, without looking, will be a dime?

A   2 out of 3

B   1 out of 5

C   1 out of 3

D   3 out of 5

34 A "quarter hour" is how many minutes?

F   4 minutes

G   15 minutes

H   16 minutes

J   25 minutes

35 To what number is the arrow pointing?

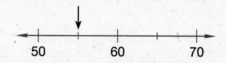

A   51

B   52

C   55

D   60

GO ON

36 An architect's ruler can measure 18 inches. How many feet is 18 inches?

F 1 foot

G $1\frac{1}{2}$ feet

H 2 feet

J $2\frac{1}{2}$ feet

37 A flag measured 72 inches long and 48 inches wide. Estimate the area of the flag by rounding to the nearest ten before calculating.

A 3,500 square inches

B 2,800 square inches

C 240 square inches

D 120 square inches

GO ON

38 Which single transformation is shown by figure 1 and figure 2?

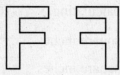

Figure 1   Figure 2

F   Translation

G   Rotation

H   Reflection

J   Not here

39 Which of the following pairs completes the table?

Number of Gallons	Number of Quarts
1	4
2	8
3	12

A   (4, 4)

B   (4, 8)

C   (4, 12)

D   (4, 16)

GO ON

40 There are 4 red tiles and 6 yellow tiles in the set of square tiles shown below. What is the probability that a tile chosen from the set, without looking, will be a red tile?

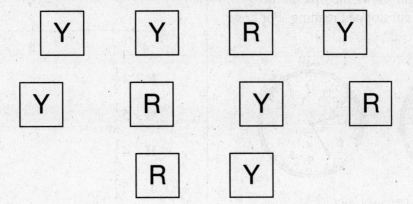

F   2 out of 3

G   2 out of 5

H   3 out of 5

J   4 out of 5

GO ON

41 The clock on the left shows the time in the morning that Raul started reading. The clock on the right shows the time in the morning that Raul stopped reading. For how long did Raul read?

A 2 hours and 30 minutes

B 1 hour and 45 minutes

C 1 hour and 20 minutes

D 1 hour and 5 minutes

42 Which fraction does point *M* represent on the number line?

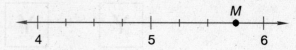

F $4\frac{1}{2}$

G $5\frac{1}{2}$

H $4\frac{1}{4}$

J $5\frac{3}{4}$

PLEASE STOP! DO NOT GO ON TO THE NEXT PAGE. STOP

Answer Document

Student's Name:

LAST												FIRST										MI

School: **Teacher:**

Fill-in your answer choice completely using a No. 2 pencil.

Samples:

A. Ⓐ ● Ⓒ Ⓓ
B. Ⓕ ● Ⓗ Ⓙ

1. Ⓐ Ⓑ Ⓒ Ⓓ
2. Ⓕ Ⓖ Ⓗ Ⓙ
3. Ⓐ Ⓑ Ⓒ Ⓓ
4. Ⓕ Ⓖ Ⓗ Ⓙ
5. Ⓐ Ⓑ Ⓒ Ⓓ
6. Ⓕ Ⓖ Ⓗ Ⓙ
7. Ⓐ Ⓑ Ⓒ Ⓓ
8. Ⓕ Ⓖ Ⓗ Ⓙ
9. Ⓐ Ⓑ Ⓒ Ⓓ
10. Ⓕ Ⓖ Ⓗ Ⓙ
11. Ⓐ Ⓑ Ⓒ Ⓓ
12. Ⓕ Ⓖ Ⓗ Ⓙ
13. Ⓐ Ⓑ Ⓒ Ⓓ
14. Ⓕ Ⓖ Ⓗ Ⓙ
15. Ⓐ Ⓑ Ⓒ Ⓓ
16. Ⓕ Ⓖ Ⓗ Ⓙ
17. Ⓐ Ⓑ Ⓒ Ⓓ
18. Ⓕ Ⓖ Ⓗ Ⓙ
19. Ⓐ Ⓑ Ⓒ Ⓓ
20. Ⓕ Ⓖ Ⓗ Ⓙ

Instructions:

1. Write your name in the space provided.
2. Be sure the problem number you are working on matches the answer number for each answer you fill in.
3. If you are taking the **Practice Test**, when you reach question 21 use the numbers in the gridded-response box.

21.

⓪	⓪	⓪	⓪	·	⓪	⓪
①	①	①	①		①	①
②	②	②	②		②	②
③	③	③	③		③	③
④	④	④	④		④	④
⑤	⑤	⑤	⑤		⑤	⑤
⑥	⑥	⑥	⑥		⑥	⑥
⑦	⑦	⑦	⑦		⑦	⑦
⑧	⑧	⑧	⑧		⑧	⑧
⑨	⑨	⑨	⑨		⑨	⑨

22. Ⓕ Ⓖ Ⓗ Ⓙ
23. Ⓐ Ⓑ Ⓒ Ⓓ
24. Ⓕ Ⓖ Ⓗ Ⓙ
25. Ⓐ Ⓑ Ⓒ Ⓓ
26. Ⓕ Ⓖ Ⓗ Ⓙ
27. Ⓐ Ⓑ Ⓒ Ⓓ
28. Ⓕ Ⓖ Ⓗ Ⓙ

29. Ⓐ Ⓑ Ⓒ Ⓓ
30. Ⓕ Ⓖ Ⓗ Ⓙ
31. Ⓐ Ⓑ Ⓒ Ⓓ
32. Ⓕ Ⓖ Ⓗ Ⓙ
33. Ⓐ Ⓑ Ⓒ Ⓓ
34. Ⓕ Ⓖ Ⓗ Ⓙ
35. Ⓐ Ⓑ Ⓒ Ⓓ
36. Ⓕ Ⓖ Ⓗ Ⓙ
37. Ⓐ Ⓑ Ⓒ Ⓓ
38. Ⓕ Ⓖ Ⓗ Ⓙ
39. Ⓐ Ⓑ Ⓒ Ⓓ
40. Ⓕ Ⓖ Ⓗ Ⓙ
41. Ⓐ Ⓑ Ⓒ Ⓓ
42. Ⓕ Ⓖ Ⓗ Ⓙ